Did You

SOUTHAMPTON

A MISCELLANY

Compiled by Julia Skinner

With particular reference to the work of Nick Channer

THE FRANCIS FRITH COLLECTION

www.francisfrith.com

First published in the United Kingdom in 2005 by The Francis Frith Collection®

This edition published exclusively for Oakridge in 2010 ISBN 978-1-84589-524-2

British Library Cataloguing in Publication Data

Did You Know? Southampton - A Miscellany
Compiled by Julia Skinner
With particular reference to the work of Nick Channer

The Francis Frith Collection
Frith's Barn, Teffont,
Salisbury, Wiltshire SP3 5QP
Tel: +44 (0) 1722 716 376
Email: info@francisfrith.co.uk
www.francisfrith.com

Printed and bound in Malaysia

Front Cover: **SOUTHAMPTON, HIGH STREET 1908** 60420p

The colour-tinting is for illustrative purposes only, and is not intended to be historically accurate

CONTENTS

INTRODUCTION

The busy modern city of Southampton stands on historic foundations. The Romans established a settlement in the area, and an Anglo-Saxon town, known as Hamwic, developed into one of medieval England's most important ports. The name evolved into Hamtun, and by the medieval period the port was known as Hampton. The name Southampton derived from Suohampton or Suhampton, probably to avoid the town being confused with Northampton. Cloth and wool were particularly important exports from Southampton, and the medieval Wool House is now a maritime museum, explaining the story of the port in fascinating detail, as does the Tudor House Museum. Important shipbuilding yards were also established in the area.

Sometimes referred to as 'the front line port', Southampton has been the embarkation point for some important military campaigns. Richard the Lionheart set sail from here for the Third Crusade in 1190; Henry V marched his troops through Southampton before they left for France and glory at Agincourt; and Southampton was a point of departure for many troops who fought on D-Day, 6 June 1944. The darker side of warfare was represented by the establishment of the Royal Victoria Military Hospital at Netley, a project inspired by Queen Victoria herself. Southampton is also famous for transatlantic cruise liners, a tradition that began when the 'Mayflower' left for America in 1620. In the great days of ocean travel all the famous liners were to be found at the Ocean Dock, among them the 'Mauretania', the 'Aquitania', the 'Queen Mary' and the 'Queen Elizabeth'; nowadays the 'Queen Elizabeth II' and the 'Oriana' can be found there. Southampton was also the home-port of the ill-fated 'Titanic', and there are several poignant monuments around the city commemorating the crew and staff who served on her, many of whom came from Southampton.

Southampton Water played a key role in the development of flying boats and sea-planes, which is superbly illustrated in the city's Hall of Aviation. Here, visitors can climb up to the flight deck of the legendary Sandringham flying boat around which the hall was built. The inside of the flying boat is reminiscent of a first class railway carriage, a classic reminder of the great days of luxury travel. Southampton Water was where these wonderful flying machines used to take off and land; it was a centre for early experimental flying and later a base for long-distance flights. The Hall of Aviation also commemorates the achievements of R J Mitchell, who designed the famous Spitfire fighter aircraft. The first Spitfire was built in Southampton, and one is on display in the Hall.

Take a stroll through Southampton today and you will find that, despite suffering heavy bombing during the Second World War, it is a fascinating mix of ancient and modern. This is a city that has much more to offer besides the sprawling docks and bustling waterfront, and this book can only give a glimpse of the colourful characters and events of Southampton's story.

SOUTHAMPTON, ABOVE BAR c1960 S151181

HAMPSHIRE DIALECT WORDS AND PHRASES

'Feeling lear' - feeling hungry.

'Cackleberries' - eggs.

'Shrammed' - cold, as in 'feeling shrammed'.

'Sherricking' - a good telling off.

'Puggled' - confused or daft, as when someone does something silly.

'Not too dusty' - when something is okay, acceptable.

'Winty' - weather that is a bit windy and a bit wintery.

'Foisty' - damp or musty.

'Ampshire Og' - Hampshire Hog, a Hampshire-born local.

HAUNTED SOUTHAMPTON

A Grey Lady has been seen by many people in the Royal Victoria Country Park at Netley. She is believed to be the ghost of a nurse who worked at the Royal Victoria Military Hospital, who accidentally killed a patient and committed suicide in remorse.

The Dolphin Hotel in Southampton's High Street is supposedly haunted by the ghost of a cleaner called Molly, who has been seen on the ground floor. Apparently she glides along the corridors with her legs below floor level.

The Mayflower Theatre in Commercial Road has a mysterious ghost, the figure of an old man sitting in a wicker chair which has been seen backstage.

MISCELLANY

Southampton Water is the wide estuary of two great rivers - the Test and the Itchen.

The 'Titanic' sailed from Southampton in April 1912. The old Terminus station is where passengers bound for the doomed ship arrived, spending the night at the majestic South Western Hotel prior to her departure the following day. A small quayside memorial marks the spot where the 'Titanic' was berthed prior to her ill-fated maiden voyage.

The statue in East Park of Richard Andrews, a 19th-century coachbuilder who was mayor of Southampton five times, was the work of Benjamin Brain, a stonemason from Shirley. The statue was unveiled in 1860, a year after Andrews' death. The inscription reads: 'As a permanent record of private worth and to honour a career of public usefulness - the fellow townsmen of Richard Andrews, five times mayor of Southampton'.

The ruined church of Holy Rood, erected in 1320 and damaged by enemy bombing on the night of 13 November 1940, was known for centuries as 'the church of the sailors'; its ruins have been preserved by the people of the city as a memorial and garden of rest, dedicated to those who served in the Merchant Navy and lost their lives at sea. There is also a memorial there to the stewards, sailors and firemen who perished in the 'Titanic' disaster.

SOUTHAMPTON, THE ANDREWS
MONUMENT 1908 60452

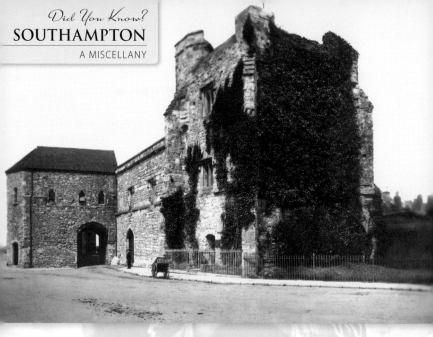

SOUTHAMPTON, THE OLD PRISON AND SOUTH GATE 1908 60429

The 15th-century God's House Tower was originally the south-east gate of the old town, and was one of the earliest artillery fortifications in Europe. The name probably derives from the Norman chapel that it contains. It is now a museum with a collection of archaeological finds.

During the Second World War there was an anti-aircraft gun on Catchcold Tower (the name of this tower is probably a nickname given by shivering guards!).

Southampton was the home-port of the 'Titanic', and many of the crew and staff were local. It has been estimated that around 500 households in the city lost a family member when the ship sank. The city has several memorials commemorating the disaster. As well as the memorial to the stewards, sailors and firemen who perished that can be found in the memorial garden of the ruined Holy Rood Church, the 'Titanic' memorial in East Park recalls the engineer-officers who 'showed their high conception of duty and heroism by remaining at their posts'. There is also a memorial to the musicians who went down with the ship, which can be found at the junction of London Road and Cumberland Place, and a touching memorial in St Josephs' Church in Bugle Street commemorates the restaurant staff who died.

SOUTHAMPTON, THE MEMORIAL TO THE RMS 'TITANIC' ENGINEER OFFICERS 1924 76259

Daniel Defoe was unimpressed with Southampton when he visited in 1722: 'Southampton is a truly antient town, for 'tis in a manner dying with age; the decay of the trade is the decay of the town.' Yet just a few years later Southampton had turned itself into a fashionable spa town rivalling Bath. The elegant Regency design and wrought-iron balconies of Portland Terrace recall Southampton's days of glory when royalty came here for their holidays.

SOUTHAMPTON, ST MICHAEL'S CHURCH 1908 60424

SOUTHAMPTON, WESTGATE 1908 60431

Henry V embarked his troops from Southampton for war with France in 1415; men passed through Westgate who went on to fight at the Battle of Agincourt. The portcullis was removed from Westgate in 1744 when it became 'a nuisance, and of no manner of use.'

On 4 October 1338, French, Genoese and Sicilian raiders successfully attacked Southampton, looting and burning the town. After this the town walls were rebuilt, in some places up to 30 feet high. The English got their revenge in 1346, when Edward III embarked his armies at Southampton for his invasion of France, and victory at the Battle of Crécy.

Jane Austen lived in Southampton between 1806 and 1809. The site of the house where she lived is now the Bosun's Locker pub in Bugle Street.

The Tudor House, overlooking St Michael's Square, is a striking timber-framed building which dates back to about 1500. It became a museum in 1911; upstairs are some fascinating aerial photographs of Southampton over the years. In the early 1980s its garden was opened to the public as a Tudor garden, which occupies a delightful hidden corner of the city.

SOUTHAMPTON, THE TUDOR HOUSE 1908 60435

Adjacent to Westgate is the Tudor Merchant Hall, which was moved from St Michael's Square to its present site in 1634, after falling into disrepair and being sold as a derelict structure - an early example of recycling. It was originally built around 1428, and housed the Woollen Cloth Hall and Fish Market. After being restored by the City Council in 1975 it is now available to hire for functions.

The Pilgrim Fathers' Monument commemorates the fact that the 'Mayflower' stopped at Southampton in August 1620 before leaving for America, via Plymouth, with the Pilgrim Fathers. The monument was erected opposite the pier on Town Quay in 1913. It is crowned by a copper model of the 'Mayflower' in the form of a weathervane.

Since 1997 Southampton University's Centre for Marine Archaeology has been investigating the wreck of Henry V's greatest warship, the 'Grace Dieu'. She was built in 1418, and at 250 feet long was about twice the size of the 'Mary Rose'; weighing in at 1,400 tons, she was by far the largest ship to be built in England at that time. In 1439 she was struck by lightning whilst at her mooring in the River Hamble, and was burnt to the waterline. The remains of the ship sank into the mud, which preserved them. The wreck was only identified as the 'Grace Dieu' in the 20th century; the University of Southampton has been investigating the site since 1970, and in 2004 joined forces with Southampton Oceanography Centre and Channel 4's Time Team to study the remains in greater detail. This has allowed the archaeologists to learn more about the medieval shipbuilders' techniques.

SOUTHAMPTON,
THE PILGRIM FATHERS' MONUMENT
1924 76265

SOUTHAMPTON, THE FLOATING BRIDGE 1908 60438

Once a year one of Britain's strangest events takes place - a cricket match played in the middle of the Solent! For about one hour each year the Brambles sandbank appears in the Solent, about halfway between Southampton and the Isle of Wight. Members of the Royal Southern Yacht Club at Hamble and the Island Sailing Club on the Isle of Wight head out to the sandbank, many dressed appropriately in cricket whites, and play a quick game of cricket before the sea reclaims the pitch. Both teams then adjourn to the Isle of Wight for a celebratory dinner.

Horse-drawn trams were introduced to Southampton in 1879, and the tram system was electrified in 1900.

Many of the medieval vaults in Southampton were used as air raid shelters during the Second World War.

This early photograph (below) shows Bargate at its best. Characterised by pointed arches and fine stonework, the old gate is also renowned for its statue of George III, gazing down the High Street dressed in classical style as a Roman and wearing a toga. Bargate is one of the finest medieval gateways in the country, dating back to the late 12th century.

SOUTHAMPTON, BARGATE 1908 60428

On the left of the photograph is the imposing Georgian church of
All Saints, built in 1795. Badly damaged in the Second World War, it

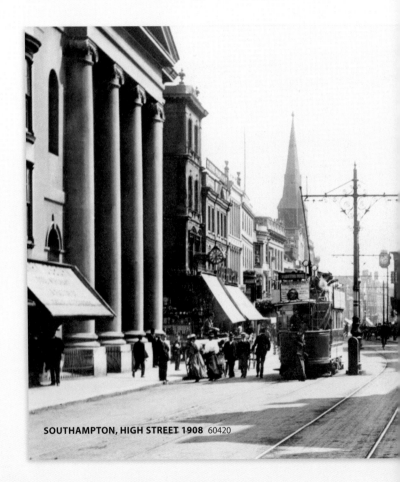

SOUTHAMPTON, HIGH STREET 1908 60420

was finally demolished in the 1950s. Jane Austen knew this church and its then minister, the Reverend Richard Mant.

SOUTHAMPTON, BARGATE c1955 S151013

By the time this photograph had been taken, the buildings on either side of Bargate had been demolished to allow traffic to pass freely around each side of it. This medieval building has witnessed the passage into the city of most of the kings and queens of England since Henry II (1154-89).

Westgate, dating back to the 14th century, provides access to the south-west corner of the old walled town. One of the finest and best-preserved of these remaining fortifications, this was once the main gate to West Quay, which for many centuries was the only quay that could accommodate larger vessels, in the days when seawater reached this far inland.

Southampton's civic centre houses one of the finest 20th-century British art collections outside London; a wide-ranging collection includes Old Masters, French Impressionists, and British 19th- and 20th-century works, including a particularly interesting group of 20th-century British portraits and sculpture.

The 3rd Earl of Southampton (1573-1603) was imprisoned for two years in the Tower of London. A portrait of him painted by John de Critz shows the Earl in his cell in the Tower with his cat, Trixie. Legend says that Trixie managed to track down her master and got into his cell via the chimney to keep the Earl company during his confinement – however, it is more probable that she was smuggled in to him.

SOUTHAMPTON, HIGH STREET 1908 60418

Until the 1930s, specially designed trams with dome-shaped tops to fit the arch travelled through Bargate. The adjoining walls and buildings were subsequently destroyed so that traffic bypassed the gate. Rounded flanking towers can be seen in the photograph on page 23, and two lions stand either side of the pointed arch.

Southampton's Common dates back to medieval times. It was purchased by the town from the manor of Shirley in 1228 for ten silver marks. Today, no other city in England has such a large area of public common, and within its boundaries more than 350 species of flowering plants and over 100 species of birds have been identified.

Southampton's famous Floating Bridge enabled foot passengers and traffic to cross the Itchen between the city and the south-eastern suburb of Woolston. The steam-powered floating bridge was in service for 141 years, between 1836 and 1977. A high-level road bridge eventually replaced it.

Founded in 1239 by the monks of Beaulieu Abbey, Netley Abbey was dissolved in 1536 and later became a private mansion. In the 18th century it passed to a Southampton builder who was killed by falling tracery as he began to demolish the site. Netley's church of St Edward the Confessor contains a medieval effigy of a crusader monk, which was found in the wall of nearby Netley Castle and probably came from Netley Abbey.

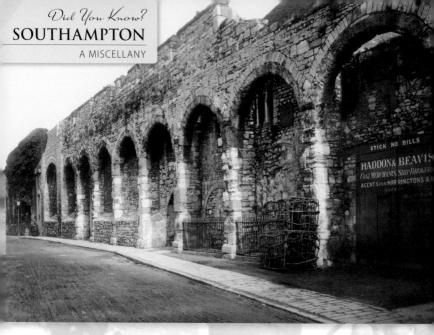

SOUTHAMPTON, THE OLD TOWN WALLS 1892 31336

Extensive stretches of the old medieval town walls survive today, and many of the towers and gates are still standing. Following the Norman invasion of 1066 Southampton became a key port, and the walls and other buildings are a permanent reminder of Southampton's wealth and prosperity in those days. Southampton's walls and defences were built from stone brought across from the Isle of Wight. This must have been a huge operation, considering that there were one and a quarter miles of walls, seven gates and 29 towers.

The first Spitfire fighter plane began her maiden flight from Eastleigh airfield (now Southampton airport) in 1936.

A complex road junction now marks the spot where the Stag Gates once stood (see below). The gates signified the entrance to the Bevois Mount Estate, and dated back to 1833. They were removed before the Second World War and their fate remains one of the city's mysteries, although the stonework may have been used in the building of the rockery by Brunswick Place.

SOUTHAMPTON, THE STAG GATES 1908 60443

SOUTHAMPTON
A MISCELLANY

This imposing building is situated on the shores of Southampton Water. The original castle, built by Henry VIII in 1542 as part of his many coastal defences, has all but disappeared, and was replaced

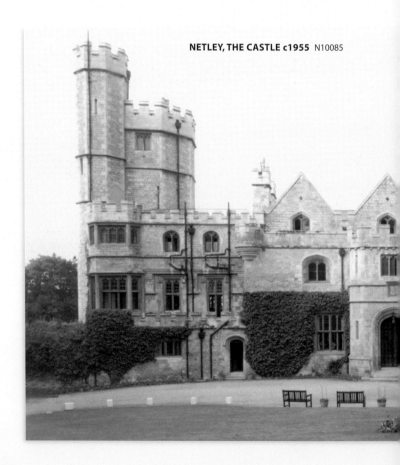

NETLEY, THE CASTLE c1955 N10085

by a large Victorian mansion during the 1880s. However one surviving relic could be the Tudor archway in the main entrance, possibly part of the old fort.

PALMERSTON

SOUTHAMPTON, LORD PALMERSTONE'S STATUE 1908 60453x

Between the 14th and the early 19th centuries Bursledon was an important centre for naval shipbuilding, with the wooded slopes of the River Hamble providing much of the timber. HMS 'Elephant', Nelson's 74-gun flagship at the Battle of Copenhagen (1801), was built here by George Parsons and launched at his yard in 1786. It was on this ship that Lord Nelson planned the battle of Copenhagen, famously raising a telescope to his blind eye. Daniel Defoe visited the area, and in his book 'A Tour through the Whole Island of Great Britain' (1722) he said of this part of the River Hamble: 'Here is a building yard for ships of war'. The church in Old Bursledon contains several memorials to former shipbuilders, including Philemon Ewer, who died in 1750. Ewer built seven large ships of war for His Majesty's service during the wars with France and Spain.

Hampshire's only commercial airport was once at the centre of a major controversy. Both Southampton and Eastleigh laid claim to its title; the problem was eventually diplomatically settled by calling it Southampton (Eastleigh) Airport.

North Stoneham Church near Eastleigh has a tombstone in its graveyard dated 1491 commemorating a group of Venetian sailors. These men may have been among the many trading fraternities visiting Southampton at that time.

The position of the Isle of Wight, which creates a sort of 'buffer', causes the Solent to have four high tides a day.

In the 9th century 20 Viking longboats were defeated by King Alfred the Great's navy in the river at Bursledon, chronicled as the Battle of Brixdone. The Viking dead are popularly believed to have been buried on what is now the site of St Leonards Church.

Medieval Southampton was an important export port for the wool and cloth trade, and the 14th-century Wool House in Town Quay Road was a warehouse. French prisoners of war were confined here during the 18th century, and some of them carved their names on the roof beams. The Wool House now houses the Southampton Maritime Museum, tracing the history of merchant shipping.

A commemorative plaque at Warsash, on the River Hamble just outside Southampton, recalls that British and Allied Naval and Commando Units sailed from the River Hamble on the night of 5 June 1944 for the D-Day landings in Normandy.

When the volcano on the tiny south Atlantic island of Tristan da Cunha blew in 1961, the entire population was evacuated to England. They were housed in the vacated RAF married quarters at Calshott until it was safe for them to return to their island.

Southampton's local legend is the story of Sir Bevis of Hampton. He fought the giant Ascapart, who was terrorising the surrounding countryside. Hanging inside the Bargate are two painted panels showing Sir Bevis and the giant.

NETLEY, THE HOSPITAL 1908 60465

Following reports of the dreadful condition of wounded soldiers in the Crimean War, it was Queen Victoria herself who originally argued the need for a military hospital, which resulted in the building of the Royal Victoria Military Hospital at Netley. The foundation stone of the hospital was laid by Queen Victoria in 1856; buried underneath it was a prototype of the newly instituted Victoria Cross decoration and a Crimea medal. Today the chapel, with its distinctive green dome, is all that remains of the old hospital, opened in 1868 and demolished in 1966. The building was an incredible quarter of a mile long. The sick, dying and injured were brought here from the war-torn corners of the British Empire, and the 570-ft-long pier enabled casualties to be carried ashore from troop ships. Unfortunately a mix-up with the plans resulted in the hospital being built the wrong way round, so that all the wards faced the sunless north; Florence Nightingale was particularly incensed by this. After the hospital was demolished in 1966, its remains were used in the building of the Totton bypass.

During the two world wars of the 20th century, more than 10 million troops left Britain through Southampton.

The vessel on the far right of the photograph below is called 'La Plata' - the name was taken by several ships from 1860 onward. These craft sailed to the West Indian islands and South America, carrying passengers and cargo. This view is typical of the kind of ships that would have been seen at Southampton's docks in the early 20th century.

SOUTHAMPTON, THE DOCKS 1917 S151002

The King George Graving Dock, included in the Western Docks, was the largest in the world when it was opened in 1933, with a capacity for vessels of up to 100,000 tons gross.

Although Southampton was made a city in 1964 it has no cathedral. Its main church is St Mary's, in St Mary Street.

SOUTHAMPTON, THE ROYAL PIER PAVILION 1908 60415

HYTHE, FLYING BOATS c1955 H372015

Langdown House at Hythe, demolished in 1963, was used by BOAC as a base for flying boats until the end of flying boat services in 1950. After the Second World War there was a drive to resurrect this romantic mode of transport, but the attempt was largely unsuccessful and these wonderful machines from a bygone era were eventually retired. The Hall of Aviation in Southampton is a must for anyone interested in learning more about them.

The famous Victorian Pre-Raphaelite artist Sir John Everett Millais (1829-1896) was born in Southampton. He was famous for painting 'Bubbles' (well-known from the Pears Soap advertisement), 'The Boyhood of Raleigh' and 'Ophelia', amongst many others. He was the youngest student ever to enter the Royal Academy. The Millais Gallery opened in 1996 in the Southampton Institute to commemorate the centenary of his death.

God's House Tower used to be the home of the town gunner, with the guns and powder stored there. During the 17th century it was used as the town jail, and prisoners of war were held in custody there.

Built by J Reid and Co of Port Glasgow in 1902, this paddle-steamer was owned by the Southampton, Isle of Wight and South of England Packet Co Ltd, and served until 1938. She was temporarily renamed 'Mauretania' in 1936 (by arrangement with the Cunard White Star Line, before the name was required for their new liner in 1937), and then again renamed 'Corfe Castle' in 1937. In 1908, the year this photograph was taken, she got into difficulties off Bognor whilst returning to Southampton from an excursion. A life-boat was called out and took off some women and children but was itself damaged and unable to continue with the rescue. Heavily beaten by the storm, the 'Queen' was eventually towed to Ryde by tug so that the remaining passengers could be safely landed.

SOUTHAMPTON, THE 'QUEEN' 1908 60457

William Shakespeare dedicated his first published poem, 'Venus and Adonis', to the 3rd Earl of Southampton, who was one of his patrons. Shakespeare's 'Henry V' dramatises the 'Southampton

NETLEY, THE ABBEY 1908 60468

Plot' against the king by Richard of Cambridge. This plot actually happened and several men were executed, including the Earl of Cambridge; their heads were displayed on spikes on the Bargate.

SPORTING SOUTHAMPTON

C B Fry must rate as one of the most extraordinary figures ever to have played for Southampton Football Club. Born in Croydon in 1872, his list of achievements is almost unbelievable. He captained England at cricket, without losing a game. In football, he played for England and was full back for Southampton in the FA Cup final of 1902. He won twelve Oxford blues, captaining the university in soccer, athletics and cricket in the same year. He also held the world long jump record for a time.

Most younger Southampton residents are probably not aware that in the early 1960s the city had a team that won the national league, and was one of the most feared in the country – the speedway team. Racing at Bannister Court, near to the old Northlands Road cricket ground, the team realised promoter Charlie Knott's dream by becoming national champions in 1962. They had a number of international stars, including three times World Champion Barry Briggs. The stadium closed just a year after the league win, and the sport has never returned to the city.

Southampton Football Club has played in four FA Cup finals, losing three and winning once. Each of these appearances has been of historic interest. In the first two final matches the club were not even members of the Football League, being in the Southern League. Unfortunately they were not able to match Tottenham's record of being the only non-league team to win the trophy. The 1976 win, over Manchester United, was famous for being one of the greatest upsets in the history of the FA Cup. The Saints had finished sixth in Division 2 that year, whilst United had finished third in Division 1, just four points behind the champions. United were also thought of as an exciting young side, and they had beaten Derby (fourth in Division 1) in the semi-final. The only (winning) goal was, ironically, scored by a Portsmouth-born player, Bobby Stokes. It was his, and the club's, finest hour - sadly, he died tragically young in 1995. The 2003 defeat, also a 1-0 scoreline, against Arsenal was notable for being the first FA Cup final played under a closed roof, the game being held at the Millennium Stadium in Cardiff.

Southampton is fortunate these days to be able to host both cricket and football in new, state-of-the-art stadia. Hampshire County Cricket Club has moved to its new home at the Rosebowl at West End, and has already hosted international cricket a number of times. It is one of only two modern purpose-built cricket grounds in the country.

Southampton Football Club moved to its new ground at St Mary's in 2001 from its former home at The Dell. It too has hosted international matches, including an England match. The new Southampton stadium is generally known as St Mary's although this is a misnomer in two ways. Firstly, the full name is 'The Friends Provident St Mary's Stadium', although for ease it is usually referred to as St Mary's. Secondly, although close to St Mary's, the stadium is actually in the Northam area. The name St Mary's is in part a reference back to the original St Mary's football club, from which Southampton Football Club developed.

QUIZ QUESTIONS

Answers on page 49.

1. Why is a hymn regularly played by the Civic Centre's clock?

2. How many Southamptons are there in North America?

3. When did Southampton become a city?

4. How many gates into Southampton were there in medieval times?

5. Why could it be said that Monaco was built on Southampton silver?

6. Bargate has been used for many purposes over the centuries. Can you name some of them?

7. How did old Southampton come to be part of modern New York?

8. The Romans had a port in the Southampton area. What did they call it?

9. Which king ate his Christmas dinner in Southampton in 1194?

10. Which popular TV detectives were played by an actor who studied at Southampton University?

SOUTHAMPTON c1900   S151001v

HIGH
CLASS
PRINTING.

HENDY'S
MOTOR
GARAGE
FIRST TURNING ON THE RIGHT

A
B
C

PORTBURY L.ᵈ

43

RECIPE

HAMPSHIRE BACON PUDDING

Ham, bacon, and pork feature strongly in traditional Hampshire recipes. Bacon rasher puddings were a popular way of using up scraps of meat, and provided a filling meal for a large family.

Ingredients:

8oz (225g) plain flour

Half a teaspoon of baking powder

Half a teaspoon of salt

3-4oz (75-100g) shredded suet

2 onions, chopped

6 bacon rashers, rinded

Half a teaspoon of dried sage

Sift the flour, baking powder and salt into a bowl. Mix in the suet, then bind with water. Roll out the dough into an oblong. Cover with the onions and bacon, leaving a margin clear around the edge. Sprinkle with the sage, salt and pepper. Dampen the edges and roll up. Tie in a cloth and boil for 3 hours, or steam, wrapped in greaseproof paper, for 3 hours.

SOUTHAMPTON c1900 S151001z

SOUTHAMPTON, THE 'MAYFLOWER' MEMORIAL c1955 S151071

RECIPE

AN OPEN TART OF STRAWBERRIES

or any Other Kind of Preserve

Strawberries have been a local crop in the Southampton/Eastleigh/Botley area for many years. Mrs Beeton had this recipe in her 'Book of Household Management'.

Ingredients:

Trimmings of puff-paste

Strawberry jam

Mode - Butter a tart-pan, roll out the paste to the thickness of ½ an inch, and line the pan with it; prick a few holes at the bottom with a fork, and bake the tart in a brisk oven from 10 to 15 minutes. Let the paste cool a little; then fill it with preserve, place a few stars or leaves on it, which have been previously cut out of the paste and baked, and the tart is ready for table. By making it in this manner, both the flavour and colour of the jam are preserved, which would otherwise be lost, were it baked in the oven on the paste; and, besides, so much jam is not required.

Time - 10 to 15 minutes.
Sufficient - 1 tart for 3 persons.
Seasonable at any time.

SOUTHAMPTON, THE CLOCK TOWER 1908 60455

QUIZ ANSWERS

1. Isaac Watts, the famous hymn-writer, was a native of Southampton. Watts wrote 'O God Our Help In Ages Past', and the Civic Centre's clock plays this hymn every four hours. There is a monument to Isaac Watts in Watts Park.

2. Seven. There are Southamptons in Massachusetts, New Jersey, Virginia, Suffolk County in New York, and two Southamptons in Pennsylvania, as well as a Southampton in Ontario, Canada.

3. Southampton became a city on 11 February 1964.

4. In medieval times there were seven gates into Southampton's old walled town. If you walk the walls today you can still see five of them.

5. Amongst the group of raiders who attacked Southampton in 1338 was the pirate Grimaldi, who used the plunder to help found the principality of Monaco. Grimaldi is still the name of the royal family of Monaco, and the wealth of the principality was partly founded on Southampton silver.

6. Bargate was originally built to guard the main road into Southampton. Over the years it has been a toll-gate, a prison, a guildhall and a museum. The original Norman arch dates back to about 1175, and the tower was added a century later. The upper floor used to be a guildhall.

7. After the Second World War, rubble from the bombed town of Southampton was taken as ballast in ships going to New York, and was used there in the foundations of Manhattan's East River Drive.

8. The Romans called their port Clausentum.

9. King Richard I, 'the Lionheart', ate his Christmas dinner in Southampton in 1194.

10. In the 1960s the actor John Nettles read philosophy and history at Southampton University. Whilst there he also acted in drama society productions, and had a lucky break when he was spotted by an agent who arranged for him to work at the Royal Court Theatre. He made his name as a Jersey detective in the 'Bergerac' TV series and now stars as DCI Barnaby in the popular 'Midsomer Murders'.

**SOUTHAMPTON, No 5 (PRINCE OF WALES)
DRY DOCK 1908** 60442

SOUTHAMPTON, ON THE COMMON
1908 60447

FRANCIS FRITH

PIONEER VICTORIAN PHOTOGRAPHER

Francis Frith, founder of the world-famous photographic archive, was a complex and multi-talented man. A devout Quaker and a highly successful Victorian businessman, he was philosophical by nature and pioneering in outlook. By 1855 he had already established a wholesale grocery business in Liverpool, and sold it for the astonishing sum of £200,000, which is the equivalent today of over £15,000,000. Now in his thirties, and captivated by the new science of photography, Frith set out on a series of pioneering journeys up the Nile and to the Near East.

INTRIGUE AND EXPLORATION

He was the first photographer to venture beyond the sixth cataract of the Nile. Africa was still the mysterious 'Dark Continent', and Stanley and Livingstone's historic meeting was a decade into the future. The conditions for picture taking confound belief. He laboured for hours in his wicker dark-room in the sweltering heat of the desert, while the volatile chemicals fizzed dangerously in their trays. Back in London he exhibited his photographs and was 'rapturously cheered' by members of the Royal Society. His reputation as a photographer was made overnight.

VENTURE OF A LIFE-TIME

By the 1870s the railways had threaded their way across the country, and Bank Holidays and half-day Saturdays had been made obligatory by Act of Parliament. All of a sudden the working man and his family were able to enjoy days out, take holidays, and see a little more of the world.

With typical business acumen, Francis Frith foresaw that these new tourists would enjoy having souvenirs to commemorate their days out. For the next thirty years he travelled the country by train and by pony and trap, producing fine photographs of seaside resorts and beauty spots that were keenly bought by millions of Victorians. These prints were painstakingly pasted into family albums and pored over during the dark nights of winter, rekindling precious memories of summer excursions. Frith's studio was soon supplying retail shops all over the country, and by 1890 F Frith & Co had become the greatest specialist photographic publishing company in the world, with over 2,000 sales outlets, and pioneered the picture postcard.

FRANCIS FRITH'S LEGACY

Francis Frith had died in 1898 at his villa in Cannes, his great project still growing. By 1970 the archive he created contained over a third of a million pictures showing 7,000 British towns and villages.

Frith's legacy to us today is of immense significance and value, for the magnificent archive of evocative photographs he created provides a unique record of change in the cities, towns and villages throughout Britain over a century and more. Frith and his fellow studio photographers revisited locations many times down the years to update their views, compiling for us an enthralling and colourful pageant of British life and character.

We are fortunate that Frith was dedicated to recording the minutiae of everyday life. For it is this sheer wealth of visual data, the painstaking chronicle of changes in dress, transport, street layouts, buildings, housing and landscape that captivates us so much today, offering us a powerful link with the past and with the lives of our ancestors.

Computers have now made it possible for Frith's many thousands of images to be accessed almost instantly. The archive offers every one of us an opportunity to examine the places where we and our families have lived and worked down the years. Its images, depicting our shared past, are now bringing pleasure and enlightenment to millions around the world a century and more after his death.

For further information visit: www.francisfrith.com

INTERIOR DECORATION

Frith's photographs can be seen framed and as giant wall murals in thousands of pubs, restaurants, hotels, banks, retail stores and other public buildings throughout Britain. These provide interesting and attractive décor, generating strong local interest and acting as a powerful reminder of gentler days in our increasingly busy and frenetic world.

FRITH PRODUCTS

All Frith photographs are available as prints and posters in a variety of different sizes and styles. In the UK we also offer a range of other gift and stationery products illustrated with Frith photographs, although many of these are not available for delivery outside the UK – see our web site for more information on the products available for delivery in your country.

THE INTERNET

Over 100,000 photographs of Britain can be viewed and purchased on the Frith web site. The web site also includes memories and reminiscences contributed by our customers, who have personal knowledge of localities and of the people and properties depicted in Frith photographs. If you wish to learn more about a specific town or village you may find these reminiscences fascinating to browse. Why not add your own comments if you think they would be of interest to others? See **www.francisfrith.com**

PLEASE HELP US BRING FRITH'S PHOTOGRAPHS TO LIFE

Our authors do their best to recount the history of the places they write about. They give insights into how particular towns and villages developed, they describe the architecture of streets and buildings, and they discuss the lives of famous people who lived there. But however knowledgeable our authors are, the story they tell is necessarily incomplete.

Frith's photographs are so much more than plain historical documents. They are living proofs of the flow of human life down the generations. They show real people at real moments in history; and each of those people is the son or daughter of someone, the brother or sister, aunt or uncle, grandfather or grandmother of someone else. All of them lived, worked and played in the streets depicted in Frith's photographs.

We would be grateful if you would give us your insights into the places shown in our photographs: the streets and buildings, the shops, businesses and industries. Post your memories of life in those streets on the Frith website: what it was like growing up there, who ran the local shop and what shopping was like years ago; if your workplace is shown tell us about your working day and what the building is used for now. Read other visitors' memories and reconnect with your shared local history and heritage. With your help more and more Frith photographs can be brought to life, and vital memories preserved for posterity, and for the benefit of historians in the future.

Wherever possible, we will try to include some of your comments in future editions of our books. Moreover, if you spot errors in dates, titles or other facts, please let us know, because our archive records are not always completely accurate—they rely on 140 years of human endeavour and hand-compiled records. You can email us using the contact form on the website.

Thank you!

For further information, trade, or author enquiries
please contact us at the address below:

**The Francis Frith Collection, Frith's Barn, Teffont,
Salisbury, Wiltshire, England SP3 5QP.**

Tel: +44 (0)1722 716 376 Fax: +44 (0)1722 716 881
e-mail: sales@francisfrith.co.uk **www.francisfrith.com**